IN THE MASTER'S HANDS

EACH LIFE SACRAMENTAL

'An outward and visible expression of
an inward and invisible grace'

WRITTEN BY **ROBERT STREET**

FOR THE *ONE ARMY* SERIES

● ALL ABOUT JESUS ● DOWN TO EARTH ● STRAIGHT TO THE HEART

First published 2016
Copyright © 2016 The General of The Salvation Army
ISBN 978-1-911149-11-8
e-book ISBN 978-1-911149-12-5
Project editor: Paul Mortlock
Design: Jooles Tostevin

Also available: *My Life in God's Hands* – an edition for
youth and young people by Nick Coke
ISBN 978-1-911149-13-2
e-book ISBN 978-1-911149-14-9

A catalogue record of this book is available
from the British Library.

Bible references are from the *New International Version*,
except where another translation is indicated in brackets.
Song references are from
The Song Book of The Salvation Army (2015).

Published by
The Salvation Army International Headquarters
101 Queen Victoria Street, London
EC4V 4EH, United Kingdom

Printed and bound in the UK by Page Bros, Norwich

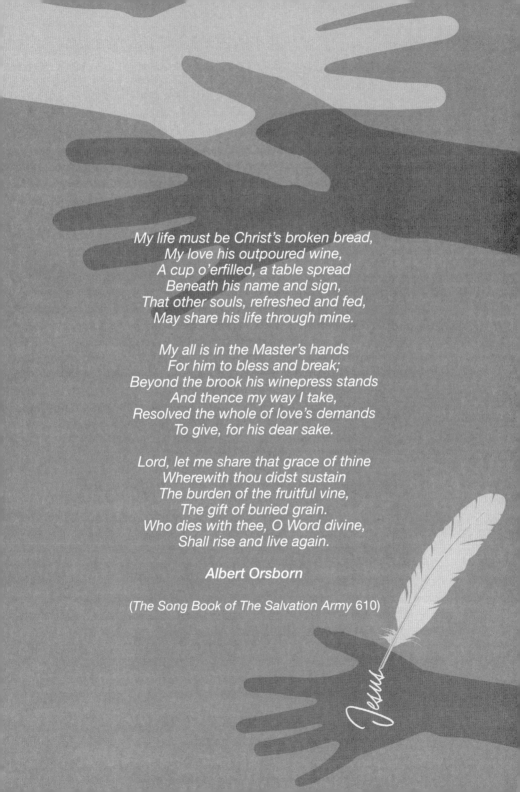

My life must be Christ's broken bread,
My love his outpoured wine,
A cup o'erfilled, a table spread
Beneath his name and sign,
That other souls, refreshed and fed,
May share his life through mine.

My all is in the Master's hands
For him to bless and break;
Beyond the brook his winepress stands
And thence my way I take,
Resolved the whole of love's demands
To give, for his dear sake.

Lord, let me share that grace of thine
Wherewith thou didst sustain
The burden of the fruitful vine,
The gift of buried grain.
Who dies with thee, O Word divine,
Shall rise and live again.

Albert Orsborn

(The Song Book of The Salvation Army 610)

CONTENTS

BEFORE WE START ...

A WORD OF EXPLANATION

What makes a Christian a Christian? What makes us what we are? What matters and what doesn't matter? Different denominations have differing answers – for all kinds of reasons. Life experience, culture, early teaching and developing convictions make us all different – everyone unique! Disagreement on these issues is hardly surprising. Yet most churches have shared values and have more in common than divides them. They sense a common bond. It is expressed in various ways throughout the world and among diverse cultures, but the bond is there. It enriches. It strengthens faith and fires mission. It can be powerful and unifying. It comes from being united in God the Holy Spirit and is something to be celebrated.

The Salvation Army's Founder, William Booth, insisted from the beginning that Salvationists should refrain from criticising beliefs and practices of other churches. It was wisdom for difficult times, when the Army found itself attacked on many fronts. His words have stood the test of time. Today, as in previous decades, the Army is glad both to encourage other Christians and to be encouraged by them. It is rich in fellowship and friendship, and it thanks God for every expression of his love in others.

In keeping with its fellowship with other churches, the Army welcomes the positive experience in Christ enjoyed by other Christians through participation in rituals or ceremonies that do not play a formal part in its own meetings. It rejoices in the strengthening of faith that occurs and is confirmed through them. It understands the value of faith expressed graciously and humbly through prayers, prose and poetry. It is in the Army's heart to do so, which means that any explanation of its own approach to worship and service, should not be viewed as denigrating the beliefs or convictions of others.

Although *In the Master's Hands* looks specifically at what being a Salvationist means, it also reflects on the place and use of specific ceremonies, observances or sacraments in the Church as a whole – some of which have caused both unity and division through the centuries. Christians the world over still have different views about them and do not always find it easy to agree on appropriate ways to deal with them.

Thus, *In the Master's Hands* has been written for Salvationists and non-Salvationists alike, conveying what the Army sees as essential or not so essential in its Christian faith and practice – and explaining why.

In doing so, it shows how the Army places the highest value on each person's inner life – their relationship with Jesus Christ. It also highlights the Army's aim to be what God wants it to be – what he called it to be – by placing itself and its people in his hands for blessing and service. One Army – in the Master's hands!

Whatever form Christian faith and practice take, and in whichever church, Christians are meant to be a reflection of Christ himself, through dedicated lives surrendered to his will. Each life sacramental – an outward and visible expression of an inward and invisible grace.

REFLECTIONS
Extracts from the script are provided at the end of each chapter for group or individual reflection. Suggestions for personal response are also offered.
Related Scripture readings are given under each heading.

The accompanying DVD may also be found online, together with the full series of *One Army* international resource teaching.

www.salvationarmy.org/onearmy

WHAT IS THE POINT?

Why become a Christian? What is the point? Why make such a far-reaching decision? What would anyone hope to achieve or prove? What might we want out of it – if anything? They are many ways in which to spend our one life – thousands of good causes to join and support. What is so special about Christianity?

It is not about having your name on a church roll, or accumulating points for attendance at Sunday meetings. It's not about helping to distinguish one person from another – Atheist, Jew, Muslim, Hindu, Buddhist or Christian. It's far more than this.

Becoming a Christian is about following Jesus. It's about learning to believe in him. It's about getting to know him, trusting him, trying to become more like him – the One who shows what a truly good life is. It's about giving your life to him. It's about developing your relationship with him, and making this relationship the foundation of your life.

It's about seeing in Jesus hope for the world and wanting to share it. It's about showing our gratitude for his unfailing love. It's about putting our life in his hands and believing it's the best thing we've ever done – the best decision we've ever made. Then discovering it really was.

SECTION ONE
IN HIS **HANDS**

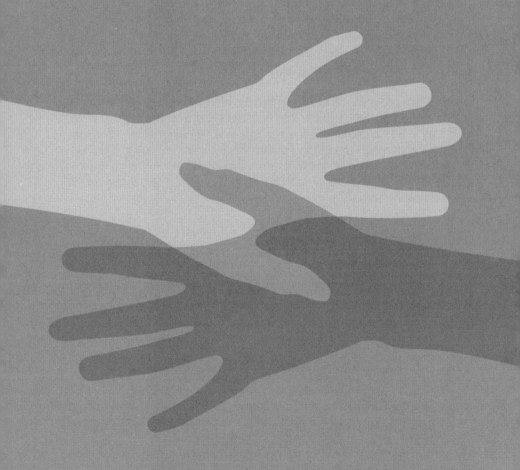

1. IN SOMEONE ELSE'S HANDS
Mark 1:16-20

How comfortable are you about being in someone else's hands? There are many ways of describing the feeling. They are varied and often in great contrast – words such as safe, vulnerable, secure, uneasy, protected, scared, loved, troubled, glad, resentful, reassured, trapped, rescued, caught and controlled come to mind. There are plenty more – all evoking emotions of one kind or another.

Not everyone finds it easy to think in terms of personal relationship with God, but the Bible demonstrates again and again how this is God's will and way for us. He wants us to enjoy it, so he invites us to place ourselves in his hands. Naturally, his invitation evokes many emotions too - and responses.

When he called his first disciples to follow him, Jesus may or may not have placed a hand on each shoulder, beckoned with a finger, or sealed the response with hands gripped in confirmation, or even a hug. We don't know. We have a few clues in the Gospels, but we aren't told to any depth what emotions were involved, or how well he already knew those he called. What we are told is that, when the call came, the first disciples responded readily and immediately (Mark 1:16-20). They left their fishing nets – and followed. They placed themselves in the Master's hands – without knowing where it would all end. They put their faith in him and trusted. No bargaining. No deals. No holding back.

It requires trust to place yourself in someone's hands. So, naturally, it requires trust – great trust – to truly place yourself in God's hands, and follow Jesus. We may wish to follow at a distance, or reserve the right to go our own way from time to time, but qualified decisions such as these only complicate matters. They don't work and diminish any true sense of being led. They also put at risk our discovering the best way forward, for the sake of wanting to control our own destiny. Jesus warned against it (Mark 8:35). The Christian life doesn't work well with half measures, nor does any relationship.

At its heart, putting ourselves in God's hands is about relationship with him. It is about being completely open with him. It is also about *choosing* to give up control. He won't snatch or force it. That isn't how he works. We are invited into the security of his hands where he promises to hold, guide and never leave us. Only as we place ourselves fully in his hands can we build

up confidence in him. When we do so, we discover the joy of working with him, learning to obey, and giving and receiving love. Following Jesus cannot help but be about relationship. It nurtures intimacy with the One who made us, who knows us better than we know ourselves, and who wants the best for us.

Albert Orsborn[1] understood this well and wrote about placing his 'all' in the Master's hands. No bargaining. No deals. No holding back.

There is no better place to be than in God's hands. There is no wiser decision than to willingly place ourselves there. It involves a step of faith, but to take it is to discover a security that stretches into eternity. It is to be where God can lovingly mould and guide us, helping us accept and understand ourselves better. It is where we are more likely to fulfil our potential and move towards becoming the people we are meant to be. The choice is and always will be ours.

In God's hands – how does that make us feel?

SHARED REFLECTIONS
'It requires trust to place yourself in someone's hands. So, naturally, it requires trust – great trust – to truly place yourself in God's hands, and follow Jesus.'

'Only as we place ourselves fully in his hands can we build up confidence in him.'

'There is no better place to be than in God's hands. There is no wiser decision than to willingly place ourselves there.'

PERSONAL RESPONSE
Use your prayer time to consider what it means for you to put yourself in God's hands and to follow Jesus.

2. JESUS IN OUR HANDS
John 1:1-14

There is something we ought to mention before we go any further. Jesus Christ put himself in someone else's hands. He who was at the beginning, who made the world and gave it life, our Creator, placed himself in other hands. Ours! The Bible says so.

In the first 14 verses of his Gospel, John explained: 'The Word became flesh and made his dwelling among us' (v 14). In doing so, God Almighty made himself vulnerable and, initially, as vulnerable as a newborn baby. It was a vulnerability that was to be cruelly exploited. Why did Jesus do it?

He did it for relationship. The apostle Paul spoke of 'God in Christ ... reconciling the world unto himself' (2 Corinthians 5:18-19 *Authorised Version*). It was divine initiative, designed to repair the broken relationship between God and us.

The first chapter of the Bible tells us that God created humankind in his own image (Genesis 1:26). It was God's intention to have relationship with us from the beginning. He gave us the earth to enjoy, and a world full of life and possibilities. He gave us the ability to relate to him and to one another. He also gave us free will. What would be the point of creating us if we were forced or programmed to obey and worship without choice? How would our relationship with him have any depth of meaning? What would have been achieved? Much of the rest of the Old Testament shows that we were not good at using our free will wisely. We abused the privilege of having personal choice. Very early on, our wilfulness brought unhappy complications and our relationship with our Creator became far from what it could or was intended to be.

We do not know precisely how, why or when the coming of Jesus was planned or decided. It is beyond our understanding to fully appreciate God wanting to share himself with us and lead us into relationship with him. Jesus spoke of a God whom we are called to worship, but whose great designs are on *our* well-being, *our* development, *our* experience and joy of life. We still seem to have difficulty in understanding and accepting such generosity of spirit.

In Jesus, God reached out to us again – readily identifying with us. Jesus shared fully in everyday life with those around him. He embraced,

protected and was advocate for the vulnerable. He could do this best by getting close to them, by being vulnerable himself. It is no surprise that John's Gospel tells us he wasn't recognised for who he was (1:10). Jesus was not God in Glory, unmoved or untouchable. He was here, human, with, for and among us in every good way.

He wasn't welcomed as we might expect the Son of God to be welcomed. John describes Jesus as not being 'received' (1:11). His vulnerability was exploited mercilessly. Treated with suspicion, he was criticised, misquoted and misrepresented. He was pursued, targeted, caught, abused and killed – undergoing all this to restore relationship with an ungrateful, unthinking, unrepentant, couldn't-care-less creation.

Jesus put himself into our hands and it seems unlikely that what happened was a surprise or shock to him. He predicted it (Mark 8:31). But by putting himself into our hands, we came to see God in a new light – serving, sacrificial, humble, supremely giving and loving, whatever our faults. Seemingly helpless on the Cross, Jesus showed mercy to those who showed no mercy to him. So we came to see ourselves in a new

light too – shameful, exposed, discredited and needing the forgiveness, mercy and grace that only God can give. We are the helpless ones.

Jesus placed himself in our hands.

SHARED REFLECTIONS

'He who was at the beginning, who made the world and gave it life, our Creator, placed himself in other hands. Ours!'

*'Jesus shared fully in everyday life with those around him.
He embraced, protected and was advocate for the vulnerable.
He could do this best by getting close to them, by being vulnerable himself.'*

'Jesus spoke of a God whom we are called to worship, but whose great designs are on our well-being, our development, our experience and joy of life.'

PERSONAL RESPONSE
Consider the vulnerability of Jesus and your willingness to trust him with yours.

3. EMPTY HANDS
Philippians 2:5-8

Jesus was God incarnate. He was God in human form. In doctrinal terms he is described as 'truly and properly God and truly and properly man'. John depicts him as the 'One and Only' (1:14 *NIV1984*). And so he was. Only Jesus could accurately be described as having 'all the fulness of God' dwelling in him (Colossians 1:19). No one else could adequately reveal the heart of God to us. Jesus did it simply and naturally by being himself.

By giving us a living picture of God, Jesus helped us see and understand the divine nature more clearly. He was here, right in front of us – breathing, talking, sharing, reacting and responding. The authority people saw in him was real and effective (Mark 1:27). It was not found in wealth, status or power, but in the virtues he displayed. John used two more words to describe him (in the same verse, 1:14). He said Jesus was full of 'grace and truth'. There were no half measures. He was *full* of them both, two supremely complementary virtues – truth to help us understand ourselves and grace to respond to whatever is revealed.

The qualities Jesus possessed meant he had insight into our failings, and understanding of how we could best be helped. They resourced him to cope with our fickleness and ingratitude, and with our refusals to believe what he knew was true and eternal (John 6:64-66). His divine nature meant he did not retaliate when ill-treated or undermined. It gave him the strength to carry on when we may have given up.

Jesus never granted himself divine 'favours'. His human trials were real. His temptations were genuine. When he was hungry he refused to use his hands to turn stones to bread (Matthew 4:1-4). He used no powers to suit his own ends. He went out of his way to embrace those who seemingly had nothing to offer him – but who needed him most (John 4:4-42). As a child, he developed naturally as any other boy, embracing the restrictions of being human. Luke puts it concisely: 'Jesus grew in wisdom and stature, and in favour with God and man' (2:52). Charles Wesley described Jesus as having 'emptied himself of all but love'[1]. He brought empty hands full of love.

Love is the key that unlocks our understanding of God. John describes God *as* love in his Letters (1: 4:8). The loving nature of God had been recognised by some Old Testament writers (Psalm 103:11-13), but in Jesus it was revealed to be deeper and greater than any of us could have dared to

hope. It was illustrated profoundly in his teaching, and it was displayed indisputably in his life – through his actions and interactions, his decisions and responses.

His human hands brought healing and comfort. They gave guidance and direction. They blessed children. He never used them to buy any one's favour or support. They washed the disciples' feet and used a towel to dry them. They were forcibly tied together like those of a criminal. Ultimately they were nailed to a cross.

Scripture encourages us to take our example from Jesus (Philippians 2:5-8). But we are not *full* of grace or truth. Our love seems weak and poor in comparison. We have virtues and qualities, gifts and some wisdom, but we are not as fully equipped spiritually as the 'One and Only'. We are not resourced to achieve all he achieved. If we try simply to copy him we will fail miserably.

But, wanting relationship with us, God is ready to help us become what he knows we can become – and offers his Spirit to help us. God in us, too.

4. WHAT WAS HE LIKE?
Matthew 9:9-13

Everyone has their own picture of Jesus. There are no photographs or first-century paintings to show what he looked like. We don't even have a written description to help us, so we are each left to our own imagination. But when it comes to information about his character, we are much better placed. There is a substantial amount of material – much of it from the mouth of Jesus himself.

We noted earlier that he acted and spoke with authority, making a strong impact with his teaching. His hearers were 'amazed' (Mark 1:27-28). Those he called to follow him identified something special about him and immediately did so. The disciples and others addressed him as 'Lord' (John 13:36-37), 'Teacher' (Matthew 19:16) and 'Master' (Luke 17:13). He was someone to look up to.

He knew how to be firm. He was strong in his challenges to those who abused their authority (Matthew 23:4), even to the point of 'driving out' the people whose money-making trading had replaced the Temple's main function of being 'a house of prayer' (Luke 19:45-46). He often clashed with religious leaders, chiding them for their sense of self-importance (Matthew 23:5-7). He disapproved of their over-burdening of people with rules and commands, and said so. He said what needed to be said, taught what needed to be taught and preached what needed to be heard.

He condemned religious leaders for promoting external religious observances while they neglected the inner things of the spirit (Matthew 23:25-28). When the Pharisees criticised his disciples for non-observance of the Sabbath, Jesus showed his displeasure at their small-minded interpretations of Scripture (Luke 6:1-5). He warned against giving organised religion too much prominence. The rules and rituals had become more important than the people they were intended to help. He was tired of people asking for signs (Matthew 16:4). The Law was available to give guidance on faith and conduct (Luke 16:29). He promoted prayer, but not pride or possessions (Matthew 6:2, 5, 9).

Jesus was not dismissive of divine commands (Matthew 5:17-20) – naturally – but it had become necessary to guide people into seeing them in their right context. Much of the Sermon on the Mount (Matthew chapters 5-7) redressed the balance between what does and doesn't matter. Jesus'

frequent use of the phrase 'You have heard' followed by 'but I say to you' indicated how priorities had become misplaced. He wanted his hearers to learn how to see beyond appearances and into the heart, where motives are found (Matthew 5:22, 24, 28). They needed to discover and then implement better attitudes and approaches.

Though people were his priority, Jesus rejected celebrity status and was never compromised by popularity. He knew how to deal with manipulation (John 7:1-6), and wasn't afraid to risk disapproval and public criticism if the well-being of others required it (Luke 19:7)[1]. Individual conversations were an essential aspect. He specifically formed relationships with 'sinful', disadvantaged and unpopular people – like the Samaritan woman, Zacchaeus, Bartimaeus and the woman caught in adultery. He didn't merely help them, he identified with them. He shared meals with them and stood up for them (Matthew 9:10-13). Such people were at the heart of why he had come to Earth – 'to seek and to save the lost', he said (Luke 19:10). Jesus readily gave himself to them.

If others rejected him or his terms of discipleship, he never used force, or even persuasion, to change their mind. He would not belittle his message by pleading with them (Matthew 7:6). He allowed them the dignity of walking away, of making their own choices (Matthew 19:22). He still does. It's the same for us.

SHARED REFLECTIONS

'He wanted his hearers to learn how to see beyond appearances and into the heart, where motives are found.'

'Though people were his priority, Jesus rejected celebrity status and was never compromised by popularity.'

'He didn't merely help them, he identified with them.'

PERSONAL RESPONSE

Consider the frequency with which Jesus challenged religious practices – and why. How does his attitude to these things affect the way you assess priorities?

5. IT'S ALL ABOUT – WHO?
John 3:16-17

But there are other attributes of Jesus we must not overlook. They are vital to our understanding of who he was and what he was like. They are at the heart of what makes relationship with him both possible and life-enhancing. They also present us with a key to unlock the door that leads us to an understanding of what we should be like too.

Jesus was unconcerned about his own importance. Paul tells us that Jesus 'humbled himself', 'made himself nothing' and took on the 'very nature of a servant' (Philippians 2:7-8). Jesus described himself in the same terms. He said he was 'gentle and humble in heart' (Matthew 11:29). At the Last Supper, when his disciples were still arguing over who was 'the greatest', he left them in no doubt that he, their Lord and Master, was 'among you as one who serves' (Luke 22:27) and washed their feet.

Religions of all kinds and many Christians have struggled with the concept of God making himself our servant. Gods are to be worshipped, obeyed and even feared. God, as Christians understand him, is almighty, omnipotent, omnipresent, all-knowing. He created the world, the universe – everything. How can it be right to call him a servant, and especially *our* servant? Surely, that doesn't make sense. It isn't logical – or even workable. But Jesus says it is!

Even so, it can be difficult for some to fully embrace the concept that we are his first concern (1 Peter 5:7)[1]. All over the world, preachers and meeting leaders can be heard during worship reminding their congregations that 'It's all about him!' They often point heavenwards to indicate they are talking about God. They want to ensure that the worship is pure and true – genuine. All praise should go to God, not to the band, worship group or preacher. We shouldn't be sidetracked into being proud of what God has made us. The honour must be given to him and him alone. There is no shortage of Bible passages to support this approach, including from the mouth of Jesus (Matthew 4:10).

That is how *we* look at things – as in our heart of hearts we want to worship our Lord worthily. But that is half the story, just as it would be only half a relationship if the communication was all one-sided. It isn't by accident that Salvation Army worship services were called 'meetings' from its earliest days[2]. They are meant to be times of communication – between us and God,

with each other, and from God to us. If we truly 'forget about' ourselves when we come before God, we miss half the point of being there. God is waiting and wanting to say things to us – to strengthen, guide and correct us. He wants us to bring our needs into his care.

Did God create us so that we would only praise and worship him? Or did he create us because he wanted to give us the gift of life, to enable us to share in his creation and so come to enjoy knowing, loving and worshipping him? Was it because, as the source of all love, he wanted to share this love, to spread it wider, to give expression to it and bless us beyond anything we could have conceived? Paul, who emphasised the servanthood of Jesus, prayed with great passion that the Ephesians would 'grasp how long and wide and high and deep is the love of Christ' and that they would come to 'know this love that surpasses knowledge' (Ephesians 3:18-19). It is the love that brought Jesus from Heaven to earth, that fired his passion to save the lost, that took him to death on a cross, that conquered the power of sin and means that still today he waits to lift us up when we fall, rescue us from ourselves and restore relationship with him.

As far as Jesus is concerned, it is all about us! He kept saying so (John 3:16; Luke 19:10). And it is to this love that he invites us to respond.

SHARED REFLECTIONS

'Religions of all kinds and many Christians have struggled with the concept of God making himself our servant.'

'Jesus was unconcerned about his own importance.'

'Did God create us so that we would only praise and worship him? Or did he create us because he wanted to give us the gift of life, to enable us to share in his creation and so come to enjoy knowing, loving and worshipping him?'

PERSONAL RESPONSE

Consider God's passion to give us the best. What does the life of Jesus tell us about the depth of love 'that surpasses knowledge'?

6. JESUS IN THE FATHER'S HANDS
Matthew 27:45-46 and Luke 23:44-46

Earlier we took time to recognise that Jesus, although God, became human and lived with us, embracing the vulnerability that goes with it. He did not excuse himself the unwelcome, unwanted, unkind or unholy side of life. Quite the reverse! He came purposely to be among us, fully identifying with his creation, and effectively placing himself in our hands. He then took the consequences.

There is another significant fact that needs to be realised. He was in God the Father's hands too. He seems to have understood this from an early age (Luke 2:41-52) when Mary and Joseph were worried because they had 'lost' him on a journey home from Jerusalem. Jesus, unlike his fretting parents, was untroubled. They found him in the Temple – which Jesus described as his 'Father's house'.

As we read the Gospels it becomes evident that not only did Jesus realise he was blessed to be in his Father's hands, but he also made sure he stayed there. He kept in constant contact and made this relationship his first priority (Mark 1:35; Luke 5:16). No one can fully understand the interaction that took place between God the Father and God the Son when Jesus was on earth, but we know that Jesus felt the need to draw strength and guidance from the relationship (Matthew 26:39). He was also committed to doing his Father's will – to obedience (John 6:38). This is a point the apostle Paul emphasised (Philippians 2:8). All this kept the relationship on a firm foundation.

Yet the strength and security of this relationship did not preclude Jesus from life's trials. Hebrews reminds us that he was 'tempted in every way, just as we are' (4:15). The Gospels tell us that Jesus was a refugee; homeless, on the run with his parents. He was despised for his goodness and honesty. He had to contend with people telling lies about him, misrepresenting what he said, accusing him of crimes he didn't commit. He was genuinely misunderstood by disciples who were slow to grasp the truth and rejected by others who decided he thought too highly of himself. Some of the saddest moments were when his closest disciples abandoned him in his hour of need – failing to pray with him and then running away (Mark 14:41, 50). He knew what it was to be alone. He also knew what it was to suffer pain in ways we hardly dare think about.

Jesus never expected to escape any of this on account of being in his Father's hands. Rather, he found the strength to bear his load because he knew he was in them. He trusted that, whatever happened, nothing could separate him from his Father. This is a theme the apostle Paul propounded with great passion. He wanted us to feel the same kind of security and certainty in God's constant love

whatever our circumstances (Romans 8:38-39). In the same way that Jesus suffered and faced his trials, so too his followers should not expect to be exempt on account of their Christian faith or commitment.

History shows that Christians have faced persecution through the ages. They still do. They have suffered from illnesses, tragedies and injustice. Jesus never promised his followers a trouble-free life, even though some over-enthusiastic evangelists may have given this unhelpful impression. Instead, he announced that he had overcome the world (John 16:33) and promised that he will always be with us (Matthew 28:20). Giving credence to every word is the fact that Jesus exercised the same trust in every circumstance – including (and especially) at his death.

The alienation Jesus felt from his Father at his crucifixion is way beyond our imagination. Taking the sins of the world – past, present and future – on his shoulders, becoming sin for us, Jesus felt utterly alone and abandoned. He cried out in anguish and told his Father so – 'My God, my God, why have you forsaken me?' (Matthew 27:46). No human experience has ever been so deep, so potentially devastating as this one – nothing, however bad, comes remotely close. Yet before he breathed his last, Jesus had the faith to say, 'Father, into your hands I commit my spirit' (Luke 23:46). His faith was not misplaced. Resurrection morning came — the world redeemed.

When Jesus invites us to trust him with our lives, to place them in God's hands, we are being invited to do so by the One who knows beyond any question what it means.

SHARED REFLECTIONS

'In the same way that Jesus suffered and faced his trials, so too his followers should not expect to be exempt on account of their Christian faith or commitment.'

'The alienation Jesus felt from his Father at his crucifixion is way beyond our imagination.'

'When Jesus invites us to trust him with our lives, to place them in God's hands, we are being invited to do so by the One who knows beyond any question what it means.'

PERSONAL RESPONSE

Consider the extent of suffering and rejection experienced by Jesus. Ask him to help you become more fully aware of his readiness to be your support when trials come – and of the fact that his choosing to suffer brings our eternal healing[1].

7. PLACING OURSELVES IN HIS HANDS
John 10:7-15 and John 17:25-26

When we look at what Jesus said and did, what his priorities were, what lengths he went to in order to make personal contact with us, and what he was determined to achieve by self-giving, we are presented with overwhelming evidence that he wants relationship with us. Nothing was too much trouble – however bad, hostile or ungrateful we may have been. That God Almighty should make himself vulnerable in the world he created is in itself remarkable, but to do so with the purpose of taking all our sins on his shoulders – past, present and those not yet committed – reveals a love beyond understanding or comparison.

What should our response be? If we want to ignore him, and make no response, he allows us that freedom. Forced love is not love at all, so he *invites* a response – a personal response.

Responses are as varied as people. Some never come close to appreciating what Jesus has done for us. Others half hear the gospel, or hear it poorly expressed, or are put off by undue pressure from parents or the bad examples of Christians, never managing to explore faith on account of these distractions. Others are just complacent or purposely avoid exploring the gospel for fear of discovering what God might require of them. They avoid any sense of spiritual struggle. Some just take it all for granted. And among those who hear and receive the good news, there are still major variations in responses. It is for each of us to make our own.

Jesus made a point of telling us that he had come to give us life 'to the full' (John 10:10) – the very best – and his sacrificial input showed that he meant it. To an utterly committed, self-giving, proactive love like this there is only one adequate or worthy response – a grateful acceptance of the gift and an utterly-committed, self-giving love in return. Such response has been described as 'total surrender' to the will of God. But herein lies the problem. It can sound overwhelming, too difficult and impossible to live up to. Because none of us is perfect we are bound to fail sometimes. The sheer magnitude of what we might be getting into provokes caution and a reluctance to promise what we may not achieve.

This is where we need to remind ourselves that Jesus is aware of that already. He knows us better than we know ourselves and he doesn't expect the impossible from us. His reason for coming to earth was to do for us

what he knew we could not, and never can, do for ourselves. As Creator he knows our limitations. He understands. So instead of expecting what we can't produce, he simply asks for our genuine wholehearted loving response – and promises to help us in that response. What happens next – and for the rest of our lives – is up to us.

The help he promises comes through our inviting him into the centre of our lives. His presence within us equips us for all kinds of circumstances. It cleanses and renews us. It gives reassurance, strength and grace. Through him we find guidance. We gain inner strength. We discover by trusting him with our life that he is true to his word, and that we are in the best and safest hands of all.

But to experience the joy of being in these hands, we must choose to place ourselves there. It is our decision to make. It involves being ready to leave behind the things that would hinder our finding the 'fullness of life' he promises. It involves being willing to let him be in control as we learn how to use our free will to best effect. And at the heart of it all is relationship – growing and developing relationship – sharing our life with him, learning how to love like him and to become more

like the God who loves us beyond anything we can understand. It is about finding and enjoying the relationship for which we were created[1].

SHARED REFLECTIONS
'To experience the joy of being in these hands, we must choose to place ourselves there. It is our decision to make.'

'We discover by trusting him with our life that he is true to his word, and that we are in the best and safest hands of all.'

'Forced love is not love at all, so he invites a response – a personal response.'

PERSONAL RESPONSE
Consider the privilege and challenge of choosing to place ourselves in God's hands. Take time in prayer to assess how fully you are doing this.

SECTION TWO
IN HIS **NAME**

8. OUTWARD SIGNS
Matthew 5:14-16

Becoming a Christian isn't meant to be a private affair. It can be personal in the sense that each decision is individually made and each relationship with Jesus is unique, but keeping the decision private misses the point.
In the Sermon on the Mount, Jesus told his followers they were 'the light of the world' (Matthew 5:14) and that they should let their lights shine (v 16). By doing so they would help others see God.

Christians are drawn together by the one Holy Spirit indwelling them. They are united in Jesus, sharing common aims and goals. In seeking to become more like him, 'family characteristics' develop and a sense of mutual support is a natural outcome. Being a Christian means identifying not only with Jesus but also with his followers. This being so, it is not surprising that we look for ways of making our faith public. We want others to know about it, and we look for the most helpful ways of making our decision formal. There are many to choose from. The important thing is to make our witness.

We can begin by telling somebody close to us – our friends and family – what has happened. We may seek out a church fellowship or have already become part of one. Through the years in Salvation Army meetings, seekers have knelt at the mercy seat[1] – a wooden bench set aside for prayer, usually sited at the front of the meeting room. There they have surrendered their lives to God and public witness has been made as they have done so – kneeling in submission and rising to new life. Many find this symbolism both helpful and significant. Other ways of testifying to becoming a Christian may take place at evangelistic rallies when an altar call is made. People are invited to 'walk to the front' if they wish to give their lives to God. Sometimes the public raising of a hand may signify a decision to 'follow Jesus'. The place and time can be significant and helpful, but it is the decision itself that matters most.

Different denominations within the Church have different ways of helping people ratify their decision publicly. Some hold confirmation services. Others baptise new Christians with water. Some do neither. The Salvation Army welcomes people into its ranks by means of a covenant ceremony for soldiers and a statement of faith for adherents. Each of these means of identifying new Christians as they publicly affirm their membership of the Church, the Body of Christ, can be useful in helping people show their allegiance to him in the presence of others. Over the years various ceremonies have been developed as different groups of Christians have

felt the need to provide something for people wanting to officially ratify their decision to follow Jesus.

None of today's ceremonies has its direct parallel in Scripture. The Early Church made its own arrangements as it grew. It left no prototype ritual or method that had to be followed. Some of the debates and disagreements that occurred as leaders tried to list what mattered and what didn't matter so much, can be found in the New Testament. They show a Church finding its way (Acts 15: 24-29) within existing cultures and not over-regulated.

Through the centuries, the temptation to infer – or prescribe – that some ceremonies are essential or more effective than others, has often been in evidence. Perhaps even without church leaders realising it, what was first intended to help people make witness to their faith has, in some cases, turned into an essential obligation to fulfil. It is unfortunate when it alienates those who may choose a different approach. In The Salvation Army both the mercy seat and its public ceremonies are seen as means of grace. They are not regarded as the only way of making public witness, or as essential steps to membership of the Church universal.

SHARED REFLECTIONS
'Being a Christian means not only identifying with Jesus but also with his followers. This being so, it is not surprising that we look for ways of making our faith public.'

'Over the years various ceremonies have been developed as different groups of Christians have felt the need to provide something for people wanting to officially ratify their decision to follow Jesus.'

'None of today's ceremonies has its direct parallel in Scripture. The Early Church made its own arrangements as it grew. It left no prototype ritual or method that had to be followed.'

PERSONAL RESPONSE
How important is it to you to let others know you are a Christian? How is it best done?

9. THE INNER LIFE
Matthew 11:28-30 and Matthew 23:25-28

As has already been acknowledged, making public witness – an outward sign – is an important step to take and plays an integral part in the life of any Christian. The inner life – where our motives, thoughts and intentions are out of sight – matters more. Jesus said so (Luke 11:37-40). He was determined to get this lesson across (Matthew 23:25-28). This brings us again to the reality of our relationship to and with God.

There is no set time in life when we become aware of God. Some are introduced to him as children and in natural ways within the 'growing up' process. Others react to what they see and hear about God, 'the Church', 'religion' or 'Christians', and form their opinions accordingly. Yet others may have been taught to be suspicious of 'God' or to discount his existence completely. Everyone has a different journey – a different understanding – and may become aware of God at different stages of life. For some, there is a great deal of 'unlearning' to do. For others, belief in God can be a confirmation of something that had always seemed to be obvious.

Whatever the case, relationship with God needs a firm foundation. At its basic level, it is not a relationship of equals. Our awareness of the almighty and loving God needs to be matched with an awareness of our humanity and failings. While God in love reaches out to us, his initiative can only be effective if we accept our need of him. Some find this easier than others. Some find humility an elusive virtue and meet any suggestion of repentance for wrongdoing with annoyance and even resentment. Only when there is an acceptance that we are all less than we could be is God able to begin work with us on making us what he knows we can become.

It makes sense to begin by placing the past in God's hands – all of it. The good things that have helped us, the unwanted things that may have damaged us, and the things we wish we hadn't done or can't put right. He takes us as we are. We simply have to come 'as we are' – with no pretence. Nothing will shock him. Nothing will surprise him. He loves and welcomes us unconditionally.

Some find it difficult to accept his forgiveness. Forgiving others can sometimes be easier than forgiving ourselves. As we give quality time to our inner-life relationship with Jesus, he waits to provide reassurance.

Having understood and done this, we can consciously place the present (and future) in his hands. There may be lessons to learn and immediate actions to take to confirm we have started a new life (Luke 19:8). There is also a relationship to cultivate and develop. So we need to give ourselves time to understand God and his ways, and to develop that understanding. Personal prayer, reading of Scripture, public worship and the fellowship of Christians play their part in this process. Gradually we can become more and more confident of God's guidance, discovering through experience that our trust in him is well placed (Matthew 11:28-30).

Having the confidence to hand over control of our lives to him varies from person to person, yet it needs to be done if we are to grow in faith. As we welcome God into the centre of our lives he shares all aspects of life with us. Nothing is hidden. He travels the path with us. But handing over control doesn't mean we stop thinking for ourselves. It doesn't negate personal decision-making and initiative. It doesn't excuse us from responsibility. Instead it means that with his promptings and direction we set out to do his will, to make a difference, to become what he wants us to become – and, importantly, to help others find him too.

The inner life is the powerhouse for all that happens on the outside.

SHARED REFLECTIONS
'Everyone has a different journey – a different understanding – and may become aware of God at different stages of life. For some, there is a great deal of "unlearning" to do.'

'As we welcome God into the centre of our lives he shares all aspects of life with us. Nothing is hidden. He travels the path with us.'

'The inner life is the powerhouse for all that happens on the outside.'

PERSONAL RESPONSE
Consider how our relationship with God depends upon our openness. How readily do you share all aspects of your life with him?

10. KEEPING IT ALIVE
Philippians 3:7-10

The original call from Jesus, 'Follow me', never changes. It is for life. Once accepted, it marks the beginning of a journey. It is an adventure in which we are led by the One who called himself 'The Way' (John 14:6). The path is his. He is everywhere before us. He knows the end and he knows what is best. We are in safe hands.

Yet it is easy for Christians to succumb to the temptation to enjoy the security while neglecting the challenge to keep moving forward – one step at a time. Unlike the risen Master whom we follow, we do not know details of the journey or the end. Instead we are urged to exercise trust.

Trust is at the heart of all relationships. Without trust they break down. We depend on one another being truthful. In our relationship with Jesus we are able to test his teaching in the Bible as we put it into practice. As he hears our words of promise he knows the depth of intention behind them. He is also ready to help us keep them.

If we are open to being guided by Jesus – to being led into situations which we cannot manage without his help – we have opportunity to prove his trustworthiness. We can grow in confidence and experience. If we shrink from being led – and stay within our 'comfort zone' – we lose out on the chance to make spiritual progress. Discipleship as such – following – is abandoned. We may still try to live by Christian values, but the growth God intends for us will not happen.

Following is a daily adventure. Our life's decision to follow needs to be put into practice each new day. It should be as natural as breathing yet never assumed as happening automatically. Daily following applies to us all – those whose vocation is within the Church, who have been on the road for many years, as well as the newest disciple. It applies to us all because each of us grows spiritually when placed in situations where only God's help will get us through. It is foolish to avoid them. Embracing them keeps our relationship with Jesus alive.

Another mark of spiritual progress, and a developing relationship, is when we begin to see ourselves as co-workers with God (1 Corinthians 3:9), ready to share in ministry and its burden (Philippians 3:10). We move on from merely thanking God for his goodness into showing our thanks by the way

we live – identifying with him when it is both convenient and inconvenient. If this development does not take place, we run the risk of expecting every personal problem to be taken away, rather than our being used by God to support others in their bewilderment and need.

As has already been acknowledged, we keep our relationship with God alive by engaging in regular prayer and Bible reading, setting aside time to be with our Master – to learn from him and hear what he says to us. It is vital to our spiritual life that we feed on him and his word. Yet engagement with 'the world' is also essential to spiritual growth. It is not enough simply to enjoy the warmth of a personal spiritual relationship without making use of it. Jesus took time to be with his Father in prayer in order to gain strength to meet the needs of those he encountered each day.

Although our relationship with God is not one of equals, we are nevertheless given opportunity to give as well as to receive. We can offer back to God the time, gifts, wealth, intelligence and abilities he has given us. In doing this, a vital dimension is added to the relationship, helping us avoid the mistake of following simply for what we expect God to give to us.

We have the dignity of choosing to contribute to this relationship – and to the lives of others – and in so doing, keeping our adventure with Jesus very much alive.

SHARED REFLECTIONS
'Following is a daily adventure. Our life's decision to follow needs to be put into practice each new day. It should be as natural as breathing yet never assumed as happening automatically.'

'If we shrink from being led – and stay within our 'comfort zone' – we lose out on the chance to make spiritual progress.'

'Another mark of spiritual progress, and a developing relationship, is when we begin to see ourselves as co-workers with God, ready to share in ministry and its burden.'

PERSONAL RESPONSE
How alive is your sense of 'following' Jesus? How does it show itself?

11. 'REMEMBER ME'
Luke 22:14-23 and Luke 23:39-43

As Jesus hung on the Cross, one of the two dying thieves hanging either side of him (Luke 23:33) asked Jesus to remember him - 'Jesus, remember me when you come into your kingdom' (v 42). The thief had nothing to offer, no gifts, not even a bribe. He didn't deserve mercy or grace, and he said so (v 41). But he dared to ask to be remembered. His request was granted – a reassuring indication of the extent, power and nature of God's all-embracing love.

The thief had no idea that Jesus himself had asked to be remembered just a few hours earlier. Jesus too was about to die – and he wanted to be remembered (Luke 22:19). Although some scholars suggest that the words 'Do this in remembrance of me,' were missing from important original texts, there is little doubt that as Jesus shared in the Passover meal with his disciples, he wanted them to understand the extent of his love for them – for all humankind – and to remember it.

The disciples were familiar with the Passover meal and its institution centuries earlier. It was held to remember how Israelites were spared death when Egyptian firstborn were killed in the night (Exodus 12:24). Lamb's blood smeared on door frames guaranteed that Israelite houses would be 'passed over' when death gripped Egyptian households. The Passover commemoration had taken place on an annual basis ever since Moses had led the Children of Israel out of Egypt and bondage.

But things would be different now. There would be something more significant to remember. Jesus was giving himself that night as the sacrificial lamb. His death on the Cross would bring salvation not just to the Jews but also to all nations and herald the redemption of creation (Galatians 3:26-29). By using Passover wine and bread as illustrations of the very real giving of his blood and body, Jesus provided powerful symbols that gave the disciples memories of that night they would never forget.

As the disciples remembered, so those who commit to him today also want to remember. At the heart of any present relationship with Jesus is our personal thanksgiving. We are forever in his debt. His sacrifice should not be regarded lightly or carelessly. By his suffering and death, Jesus did for us what we had proved incapable of doing for ourselves. He took responsibility for all our wrongdoing – all that alienates us from a righteous God – and reconciled us and our world to him (2 Corinthians 5:18-19). To forget or neglect this would be to fail in our understanding of our worth to God and his love for us.

Although the Passover was an annual remembrance, it wasn't long before the early Christians wanted to remember the Lord's death on a frequent basis. It seemed natural to do so, especially at meal times. This is something that Christians through the ages – including Salvationists – have continued to do, both at home and when meals are shared within Christian fellowship[1]. Such practice keeps the remembrance alive. It is not an annual event or an occasional commemoration, but part of everyday life – much as it was with the Early Church (Acts 2:46).

A few years ago, when The Salvation Army's International Spiritual Life Commission (ISLC)[2] presented 12 calls to Salvationists, it advocated a wider use of fellowship meals and gave a variety of examples[3] of how such occasions could be used to enrich corporate life. In doing so it recognised the 'freedom to celebrate Christ's real presence at all meals and in all meetings'. Most important of all, by welcoming Christ into the centre of their lives, Christians are able to celebrate Christ's real presence in their hearts at all times and in all places. There is no more effective way to remember him – and his sacrificial love.

SHARED REFLECTIONS
'There is little doubt that as Jesus shared in the Passover meal with his disciples, he wanted them to understand the extent of his love for them – for all humankind – and to remember it.'

'He took responsibility for all our wrongdoing – all that alienates us from a righteous God – and reconciled us and our world to him. To forget or neglect this would be to fail in our understanding of our worth to God and his love for us.'

'Most important of all, by welcoming Christ into the centre of their lives, Christians are able to celebrate Christ's real presence in their hearts at all times and in all places.'

PERSONAL RESPONSE
Consider our desire to remember Christ's sacrifice for us. How do we best show our thanksgiving?

12. CHRIST'S REAL PRESENCE
Ephesians 3:16-19 and Colossians 1:24-29

The presence of Christ in the life of a believer is a blessing beyond words. He comes by invitation (Revelation 3:20), and makes our hearts his home. He comes with the intention of staying, to be our constant companion and guide. Paul describes this as 'Christ in you, the hope of glory' (Colossians 1:27). He stays to help us with our trials, raise us up when we fall and keep us in his grace. We can be confident of his love.

We acknowledged earlier the folly of taking his presence for granted and the importance of keeping the relationship alive. The new spiritual birth that comes when we are 'born of the Spirit' (John 3:3-8) paves the way for spiritual growth, development and maturity. The development takes place within the security of an ongoing relationship in which Christ's inner presence is a reality – unseen, unheard but constant (Ephesians 3:16-19). His presence is not guaranteed by ceremonies or rituals but is determined by our willingness to welcome him. It also speaks of the immediacy of grace.

In the early days of the Church, when it was new and finding its way, the concept of sacrament didn't exist. The word 'sacrament' is not found in the Old or New Testaments. It began to emerge towards the end of the second century, opening the door for rituals that were close to those found in some other religions[1]. Initially, the breaking of bread and remembrances of the Lord's death had been 'thanksgiving' occasions, somewhat unregulated without the need for an apostle or bishop to preside[2]. They were natural expressions of love and worship of the Lord. In AD 110, Bishop Ignatius announced that baptisms and love feasts should not take place without a bishop[3]. Later, with the introduction of the concept of sacrament[4], and other changes, the Church started to look quite different. Whereas the Lord's Supper had been a meal (as the name suggests), a move towards the remembrance becoming a separate ritual took place.

What was emerging was something different in form from the Last Supper Jesus had shared with the disciples. Rituals were bringing order and obligation. Church leaders were, not surprisingly, introducing power and control. As year succeeded year and centuries of worship developed, it was inevitable that some rituals would become rites of incorporation into the Church.

History records many disputes and arguments among different groups, leading to tragic splits within the Church, including over what constituted the real

presence of Christ in the life of a believer. Gradually, a concept took shape that Christ's actual presence was in the elements used in the Eucharist. This in turn led to a belief that Christ himself is 'received' by communicants each time they partake in the service. It is not a view held by all who partake in Communion services, and the understanding and experience of each believer can vary widely. Many testify to such moments being deeply precious with a real sense of closeness to God. They can be profoundly significant in different ways for different Christians – but the rituals in themselves are unable to guarantee Christ's presence in a person's life. Sincerity of heart and daily openness to Christ confirm his presence – both in Spirit and truth (John 4:24).

During the first millennium a wide variety of pronouncements emerged as to the nature of the wine and bread used in the sacrament, but it was not until the late 11th century that the term 'transubstantiation' seems to have been officially embraced[5]. Transubstantiation is defined as 'the change by which the bread and wine offered in the celebration of the sacrament of the Eucharist become, in reality, the body and the blood of Jesus Christ'. Different communions interpret this and similar concepts in differing ways, but the defence

and rejection of this position in the second millennium have been responsible for great misery, division and even killings through the centuries. When Jesus asked his disciples to 'do this in remembrance of me' we can be sure he did not have such outcomes in mind.

Fortunately, this is not the full story.

SHARED REFLECTIONS

'The presence of Christ in the life of a believer is a blessing beyond words.'

'He stays to help us with our trials, raise us up when we fall and keep us in his grace.'

'His presence is not guaranteed by ceremonies or rituals but is determined by our willingness to welcome him. It also speaks of the immediacy of grace.'

PERSONAL RESPONSE
Consider the presence of Christ in each heart that welcomes him and the natural, personal bond this establishes. What doors does this open for your daily living?

13. BEING TRUE TO SCRIPTURE
John 13:34-35

One of the sad features of disputes in the Church over what Jesus meant and how his real presence is enjoyed, is that generally those involved have been trying to be true to Scripture. The problems have come when anyone, or any one denomination, has not only been convinced that their interpretation is right, but also that others should be prevented from holding or celebrating an alternative view. It introduces exclusiveness, preventing other Christians from joining in specific forms of worship.

There should be no surprise that differing opinions emerge, especially between cultures and age groups, and because of varied intellectual understanding. We are all different – every one of us is unique. We have been created with the ability to think, decide and act for ourselves. No one has been created with the capacity for knowing all things (1 Corinthians 13:9-12), or for always being right. The differences we enjoy – in gifts, thought and convictions – can be used to enhance one another's lives. They need not lead to confrontation.

The number and variety of ways in which the death of Jesus is remembered are endless. The understanding of what takes place in particular ceremonies and in different churches is profoundly wide. The sheer variety of understanding (and disagreement) over some rituals and other forms of worship, means there can be no automatic assumption that what takes place in any one setting is of itself being true to what Jesus intended. (Even so, there are those who unquestioningly seem to assume so, perhaps without thinking this through.)

There were disputes over forms and places of worship when Jesus was on earth, and his response couldn't have been clearer – 'God is spirit, and his worshippers must worship in the Spirit and in truth,' (John 4:24). No site, ceremony, ritual or service matters *in itself* – with or without symbols. What matters is the spiritual response in each heart. The unity felt in Christ and with his people (of whatever denomination) can be powerful and spiritually enriching when worship is offered in this way. In countless denominations the world over and through the ages, Christians have discovered the strength of being united in Christ when 'Spirit and truth' are at the heart of what takes place. The bond that links them together is found in the sacrificial love of Christ, and this brings the kind of unity of which Jesus spoke (John 13:34-35).

Just after Jesus had washed his disciples' feet, and set them an example of humility that he told them to remember and emulate (John 13:12-17), he re-emphasised what this lesson was really about. They should love one another. In the same way that the disciples missed the point of discipleship by arguing

about who was the 'greatest' – even when they were in the upper room – Christians have since been in dispute over ceremonial ways in which the New Covenant should be expressed; what Jesus meant, may have meant, or didn't mean. Sadly, in doing so it is possible to miss the real point of it all.

Jesus had affirmed that the two great commands were to love God with all our heart, soul, strength and mind, and our 'neighbour' as ourselves (Luke 10:27-28). There were no 'ifs' and 'buts' about this. Love matters most and the way we treat each other shows whether our hearts are right. In the upper room, Jesus spoke to them yet again of his example and their need to follow it – 'As I have loved you, so you must love one another' (v 34), he commanded. They knew the command to love was the greatest command. Now he commanded them to love *as he loves*.

We love by being inclusive, not exclusive, in our worship. We love by being welcoming and all-embracing – as he was. The Salvation Army's longstanding motto, 'With heart to God and hand to man' has, for years, been an aspiration to live by the two great commands. Its public worship meetings and service to humankind are intended to be open to all. Its openness to its own members participating in other churches' services, whenever welcomed, further supports its desire for inclusiveness and unity[1]. Essentially, it promotes a simple and uncomplicated stance that opens doors. The Army was called to be inclusive, serving and welcoming.

The freedom the Army enjoys to remember the Lord's death in any number of creative and inclusive ways is something to be treasured and put to full use[2] – in worship and service. Whenever it does so, it is being true both to Scripture and to the obedience Jesus requires most of all – the command to love.

SHARED REFLECTIONS
'There should be no surprise that differing opinions emerge, especially between cultures and age groups, and because of varied intellectual understanding. We are all different – every one of us is unique.'

'No site, ceremony, ritual or service matters in itself – with or without symbols. What matters is the spiritual response in each heart.'

'They knew the command to love was the greatest command. Now he commanded them to love as he loves.'

PERSONAL RESPONSE
Consider how the command to love is greater than other commands and that in obeying this command we show most respect and thanksgiving for all that Jesus has done for us.

14. THE BODY OF CHRIST
1 Corinthians 12:12-13 and Ephesians 4:4-6

There is only one Church – just one. Christians call it the Body of Christ[1]. There can be only one. It is not a human invention, nor is it dependent upon any ecclesiastical structure. It is of the Spirit; invisible, unseen. It comprises all who confess Jesus Christ as Saviour, who welcome him as Lord of their life, and are thus united in the Holy Spirit. That unity is emphasised by the apostle Paul in his First Letter to the Corinthians (12:12-13), where we read: 'The body is a unit, though it is made up of many parts; and though all its parts are many, they form one body. So it is with Christ. For we were all baptised by one Spirit into one body – whether Jews or Greeks, slave or free – and we were all given the one Spirit to drink' (*NIV1984*).

Paul continues this theme in his letter to the Ephesians (4:4-6), where we read: 'There is one body and one Spirit, just as you were called to one hope when you were called; one Lord, one faith, one baptism; one God and Father of all, who is over all and through all and in all.' The verses speak of all things being united in Christ. There is no sense of division. There is no mention of ecclesiastical structure.

Yet although the Church is essentially made up of people, it isn't possible to avoid the human need for structure and order. Through the centuries the Church has emerged in many forms. Within the varied circumstances of many generations and situations, churches began to assume specific identities. With their emergence came creeds, statements of belief, various codes of practice and obligations to be fulfilled. Often churches found themselves largely in agreement with one another's emphases. Denominations took root with specific requirements for membership. Sometimes they found themselves in disagreement with each other, with any sense of unity in the Body of Christ being lost.

The Acts of the Apostles tells us that when the Church was new (and comparatively small) 'all the believers were one in heart and mind' (4:32). As the Church grew and collected more and more people, it also attracted a greater diversity of views and convictions. It is not difficult to understand why, 2,000 years later, the Church is represented by a multiplicity of denominations. Yet none of these – including The Salvation Army – is in itself the one true Church. No church history is so pure or uncorrupted as to set it apart from others and assume God's special favour. Each church or denomination may be an *expression of the one true Church*, but no more.

The same principle applies to ceremonies or practices for the initiation of new members into a church – and by implication recognising membership into the Body of Christ. Baptism into the Body of Christ happens by being 'born of the Spirit'. Paul's words, 'we were all baptised by one Spirit into one body', reminds us of this. Our being born into the Kingdom of God takes place when we open our hearts to the Lord (Acts 11:15-17). It cannot be guaranteed by any ceremony, however moving or inspiring. Paul's emphasis that there is only 'one baptism' by 'one Spirit' shows that no particular form of baptism is obligatory or essential[2]. All initiation ceremonies can be helpful and God-blessed, but we must guard against giving them an importance they do not merit. The Church cannot control the Holy Spirit's initiative and activity.

This seems to be a constant message from Paul who, as well as showing his concern that some public baptisms already had the wrong emphasis (1 Corinthians 1:13-17), chastised the Galatians (3:3) for moving away from 'the spiritual' and returning to old ritualistic practices. It seems our natural tendencies for regulation and order need to be reviewed from time to time. Our place in the Kingdom of God, our belonging to the Body of Christ, our membership of his Church, are sealed with countless others, by the giving of ourselves to him as we welcome him as Lord. As we place our lives in his hands we can be sure of his acceptance and blessing.

SHARED REFLECTIONS

'There is only one Church. Christians call it the Body of Christ. There can only be one ... It comprises all who confess Jesus Christ as Saviour, who welcome him as Lord of their life, and are thus united in the Spirit.'

'Each church or denomination may be an expression of the one true Church, but no more.'

'All ceremonies can be helpful and God-blessed, but we must guard against giving them an importance they do not merit. The Church cannot control the Holy Spirit's initiative and activity.'

PERSONAL RESPONSE
Consider the frequent use of the word 'one' from Scripture in this chapter. How is your 'oneness' in the Body of Christ confirmed?

SECTION THREE
IN HIS **LIKENESS**

15. BECOMING LIKE HIM
2 Corinthians 3:17-18

We earlier took a brief look at what Jesus was like. We glimpsed his character from the Gospels. By becoming like us (Romans 8:3) he made it possible for us to see the heart of God in ways we can understand. And because he became like us – embracing humanity – we can see more clearly what it might mean for *us* to become like *him*.

Our becoming like him is a constant New Testament theme and hope. It is not just a nice idea but is presented as the fulfilling outcome of our relationship with God (1 John 3:2-3). Paul describes those who 'turn to the Lord' as 'being transformed into his likeness' (2 Corinthians 3:16-18). Why is becoming like Christ so important? Why is it presented as the ultimate aim of life?

One simple, clear answer is that there is no better example of how to live. We may admire some people and applaud our heroes, but even the best of those falls short of an ultimate standard for living. Jesus is described in Scripture as 'without blemish' (1 Peter 1:19) and 'without sin' (Hebrews 4:15 *ESV*). As we noted earlier, John presents Jesus as 'full of grace and truth' – something that is true of no one else.

Why should we accept these statements without having met the man Jesus for ourselves? What might lead us to think such claims are true? Brief though the Gospels are, and with such a small number of words, they nevertheless make compelling reading with their consistency over who Jesus was, what he taught and how he lived. When each of these aspects of his life are examined or scrutinised, they hold together. There is a unique integrity about them. What Jesus preached, he lived out with a consistency that no other teacher has come near to emulating. The things he taught – when we put them into practice – prove their own worth. The truth of his words becomes self-evident when they are applied.

He never demanded of others what he wasn't prepared to do or give himself, yet he also made allowances for other people's weaknesses and failures. He gave remedies for starting again and encouragement to go with them.

Those who thought his theories or integrity might break down when the going became tough, were proved wrong. When things turned ugly and he

was abused, defamed, misjudged and condemned to death, they discovered that the reverse was the case. Everything he had taught about selflessness, surrender, giving and forgiving, was confirmed in his responses. The way to life was not found in human power bases, force, manipulation or even supreme skill or intelligence. It was found through and in love.

In Jesus fullness of life is seen in his humility, goodness, self-giving and love. Jesus never professed that doing God's will and living for others would be easy or prevent hardship and disappointment. Instead he taught that selfless living, with all its challenges, ultimately leads to fullness of life (Mark 8:35). Those who find the courage to trust him as they seek to do so, also find a divine quality of companionship and strength that cannot be found elsewhere.

All of us need examples to follow, even if sometimes we are reluctant to admit it. We are lesser people without goals to aim for and aspirations to make progress. This particularly applies to our inner life, to intentionally looking to become a better person – someone wanting their life to make an impact for good, to make progress in ways that speak of God's guiding and goodness.

There are those who choose to 'opt out' or give little thought to this. But for those who want to become the person God intends for them, there is no better aspiration than to live to become more like Jesus.

SHARED REFLECTIONS

'Because he became like us – embracing humanity - we can see more clearly what it might mean for us to become like him.'

'Our becoming like him is a constant New Testament theme and hope. It is not just a nice idea, but is presented as the fulfilling outcome of our relationship with God.'

'What Jesus preached, he lived out with a consistency that no other teacher has come near to emulating. The things he taught – when we put them into practice – prove their own worth. The truth of his words becomes self-evident when they are applied.'

PERSONAL RESPONSE

Our becoming like him is described as 'being transformed'. What does this mean for you?

16. WHAT DOES IT MEAN?
1 John 3:23-24

No two people wanting to become more like Jesus begin from the same place. Everyone has a different starting point. But, whatever our circumstances, Jesus starts with us where we are. We are not on our own.

It helps immeasurably to know that Jesus didn't come to condemn us. He came to save us. He said so (John 3:17). It helps because the starting place for some people on the journey towards Christlikeness is a long way back. Some have known only corruption in their cultures and upbringing. Embracing new values and changing behaviour is not achieved overnight. Some have been abused or unloved from birth. Others have been oppressed or had confidence knocked out of them. The healing process necessarily takes time. Jesus knows all this and more, of course. In our quest to become more like him we need to have patience and understanding both with ourselves and with one another – the kind of patience he has with us.

A major factor in becoming like Jesus is that we don't become more like him by trying to copy him. We become more like him by inviting his Spirit into our lives and asking him to mould us into the person he knows we can be (1 John 3:24). As we have emphasised before, his presence makes all the difference.

His presence also means he will show us things about ourselves that we may not have previously realised. We will become more aware of our need for improvement. As we become more ready to admit our shortcomings we become less ready to condemn the faults of others. A transformation has begun, but not everyone copes well with changes of this kind, so it is important to keep open to what needs to be 'given up' or surrendered – as well as to what can be developed. In the busyness of life this is not always easy to achieve. There are many distractions, with plenty of excuses available for failing to follow through our first intentions.

One of the most problematic of hurdles can be obedience. For some, an inbuilt resentment to 'being told what to do' results in failure. For others it may be a sense of 'losing control' – not recognising that God never forces his control over our free will. His influence is by our invitation and still leaves decisions with us. It is, nevertheless, a crucial aspect of discipleship. It requires humility to follow – and humility is not always the most natural of character traits.

Obedience and humility are two of Jesus' characteristics that Paul points to when he is describing Jesus to the Philippians (2:8). At the same time he presents Jesus as a servant – not as someone who had servanthood forced on him, but as someone who chose it in order to save us (v 7). Becoming like Jesus involves our embracing a life of service for the sake of others. This applies to leaders too. Leaders are called to serve God and their people – not to feel important (1 Peter 5:2-3). Salvationists are 'Saved to Serve'.

In encouraging the Philippians to become more like Jesus, Paul urges them to have the same attitude as Jesus (2:5). We develop that attitude through Christ's inner presence. It can't be done without it. Paul shows that obedience, humility and servanthood are evidence of that attitude, but we best sum it up by recognising that Jesus lived for others – us – with no discrimination. The Church, The Salvation Army, any organisation, can produce the most brilliant plans, but without the right attitude everything can fall to pieces. 'Your attitude should be the same as that of Christ Jesus' (Philippians 2:5 *NIV1984*), says Paul. For anyone seeking to become like Jesus, that sums it up well.

SHARED REFLECTIONS

'We become more like him by inviting his Spirit into our lives and asking him to mould us into the person he knows we can be.'

'In our quest to become more like him we need to have patience and understanding both with ourselves and with one another – the kind of patience he has with us.'

'It requires humility to follow – and humility is not always the most natural of character traits.'

PERSONAL RESPONSE
How can I differentiate between God's Spirit within me and trying hard to be good? How can my 'attitude' become more like Christ's?

17. SAVED TO SERVE
Matthew 25:31-46

When General Albert Orsborn wrote the song 'My life must be Christ's broken bread', he highlighted the place of commitment in Christian service. The song[1] speaks of ready surrender to God's will and, in the second verse, uses the analogy of a Christian being bread in Christ's hands. It highlights that anyone placing themselves there does so 'for him to bless and break'. We are to be used in his service.

The song has been described as 'sacramental'. The description fits if we apply the generally accepted basic definition of a sacrament as 'an outward and visible sign of an inward and invisible grace'[2]. Empowered by his Spirit, our lives offer outward evidence of his grace within. Our faith is expressed by the way we live. Discipleship is not meant to be self-centred. The grace we are given is to be shared. Jesus told the disciples, 'Freely you have received, freely give' (Matthew 10:8). It is the same for us.

The song demonstrates total commitment. The first verse uses words that speak of being broken, of being filled to overflowing, and of love being poured out. There are no half measures – and the placing of ourselves into God's hands is all for a far-reaching, God-glorifying purpose. The verse concludes: 'That other souls, refreshed and fed, may share his life through mine.' Having found the blessing of God we are to help others find it too. We are saved to serve.

We serve people best when we see them as equally loved by God. We all stand in need of God's forgiving grace. If we have any virtue it comes by the grace of God. It is not something we have earned or that entitles us to feel superior to those to whom we minister. As for service to God, it can be given in many forms.

In the parable of the sheep and the goats, Jesus was uncompromising about our duty to help the disadvantaged – those who are hungry or thirsty, without clothing, strangers, unwell or in prison (Matthew 25:31-46). He taught that we should treat them as well as we would treat him – 'whatever you did for one of the least of these brothers and sisters of mine, you did for me' (v 40), he said, adding, 'whatever you did not do for one of the least of these, you did not do for me' (v 45). In the same way that he identified fully with them by referring to them as 'these brothers and sisters of mine', so we are to identify with them – and not take a superior stance.

The Salvation Army's ministry to the disadvantaged is known throughout the world. The volume and variety of its caring ministry is an ongoing reminder that we are 'saved to serve'. It can almost be taken for granted. We can be tempted to rest in the knowledge that 'the Army' is carrying out a massive organised ministry to the disadvantaged – and forget our personal loving obligations. Every day of our lives, loving God and loving others involves our commitment to be to others whatever is needed at the time.

We show the depth of our Christianity (or lack of it) by the way we react to or ignore others, by our indifference or compassion, our self-centredness or self-giving. It is easy to fall into the false ideology that our own happiness should be our first concern. If we do so, the demarcation lines between those who profess to follow Jesus and those who don't, cease to exist.

Jesus told his disciples to 'freely give' just after he had given them authority to act in his name (Matthew 10:1). When he empowers or equips us to act in his name it is in order that we can better serve others – and above all help them find Jesus too. The authority he gives us is to serve[3].

SHARED REFLECTIONS
'Discipleship is not meant to be self-centred. The grace we are given is to be shared.'

'We show the depth of our Christianity (or lack of it) by the way we react to or ignore others, by our indifference or compassion, our self-centredness or self-giving.'

'We serve people best when we see them as equally loved by God … If we have any virtue it comes by the grace of God. It is not something we have earned or that entitles us to feel superior to those to whom we minister.'

PERSONAL REFLECTION
Consider all that you have 'freely received' from Jesus. In what ways do you fulfil his instruction to 'freely give' what you have received?

18. SACRAMENT
Romans 12:1-2 and Galatians 5:1-6

We noted earlier that the word 'sacrament' cannot be found in Scripture. It is not a concept with which Jesus' disciples were familiar. Jesus is not recorded as using the word at any time, including at the Last Supper. It played no part in the life of the Church of the first century. The concept of the sacramental, which included drawing together baptism and the breaking of bread, emerged later – with rituals, order and obligations that were not part of New Testament life[1]. Contemporary sacramental observances – of whatever kind – are the outworking of various churches' understanding over time, rather than a direct application of what Jesus said. Yet the word 'sacrament' has become meaningful to Christians everywhere, if not always with the same understanding or implications.

The concept of 'sacrament' (*sacramentum*) in Christian circles emerged at the end of the second century as a way of comparing newly-instigated rituals with those of other religions. As it did so, it ran the risk of detracting from the more important concept of the mystery of God (*mysterion*), which Paul describes as 'Christ in you, the hope of glory' (Colossians 1:27).

Jesus wanted his disciples to understand the potential of 'Christ in you' and promised that he would send the Holy Spirit to be with them – and us (John 16:7 and 17:20-21). When Jesus chose to be baptised in the Jordan (away from religious officialdom) there was no sense of his needing to repent of sin – John the Baptist was alarmed at the thought of Jesus being baptised at all (Matthew 3:13-15). But the occasion introduced a new emphasis that, whereas John had 'baptised with water', Jesus would 'baptise with the Holy Spirit'[2] (Luke 3:16). These words are recorded in each of the Gospels and are also among the last recorded words of Jesus after his resurrection (Acts 1:5). They have far-reaching significance. Jesus had come to plant God in the hearts of his created people, through his Spirit. Their daily living would confirm his presence and be seen in their actions.

Later on, Paul put this into context when he urged Christians in Rome to 'offer your bodies as a living sacrifice, holy and pleasing to God' (Romans 12:1). We best honour God by the way we live, he said – this is the kind of worship or service God requires. Ritual or ceremony does not give it authenticity. Authenticity comes through demonstrating the sincerity of the offering on a daily basis. Essentially it is given credence by 'Christ in you'.

Nevertheless, it is within human nature to establish agreed procedures, to want guidelines and fixed ways of expressing shared beliefs or aims. When Peter, James and John witnessed the transfiguration of Jesus, they wanted to

commemorate the event by building three shelters in honour of Jesus, Moses and Elijah (Mark 9:2-8). Today specific occasions are marked throughout the world and in all religions with ceremonies that bring people together. There is a place for them in societies of all kinds. They help us give substance to what is spiritual.

When sacramental observances were developed they took on a special importance of their own. They were perceived as essential or somehow seemed more significant or worthy than other forms of worship. God-blessed though they can be, there is no suggestion from Scripture for any assumed superiority. As we have noted before, Jesus consistently taught that what happens inside a person matters far more than that which happens on the outside. It is his presence within us that matters, however we may choose to affirm it.

None of this negates the value of ritual or ceremony, nor does it proscribe the multiplicity of ways in which God may be worshipped and his name honoured. However, it does indicate that spending much energy and time on debating how sacraments relate to any denomination's standing in the Church, fails to grasp that salvation is not achieved by such obligations. The same can be said for 'Christian unity', which is essentially of the Spirit.

Having looked at the way some Christians were returning to Jewish ritual, and seeing it as essential, the apostle Paul chastised them and asserted with strong authority, 'The only thing that counts is faith expressing itself through love' (Galatians 5:6). It is a lesson that needs to be continually remembered.

PERSONAL RESPONSE

Consider how easy it is for Christians of all denominations (including Salvationists) to put faith in ceremonies and specific achievements, rather than in the saving work of grace Christ does in our hearts.

19. CHRIST – THE ONE TRUE SACRAMENT
John 1:14; 2 Corinthians 4:5-6 and Colossians 1:27

The widely accepted definition of a sacrament as 'an outward and visible sign of an inward and invisible grace' is attributed to St Augustine. This means it has been used and interpreted in various ways since the fifth century.

As we have already noted, Jesus taught that the inner motives of our heart matter more than any outward show of religion (Matthew 6:16-18). Our inner thoughts and decisions mould the people we become and are usually evident by the way we live – but not always. There are times when we hide our real 'self' from others.

It was different with Jesus. He came purposely to reveal God to us. What was seen on the outside came from the heart of God on the inside. There was no falsehood, no pretence, no deception. To look at the human Jesus was to see the divine God. John describes this as 'the Word made flesh' (1:14) adding, 'We have seen his glory, the glory of the One and Only, who came from the Father, full of grace and truth' (*NIV1984*). Paul said much the same, and wrote of 'the light of the knowledge of the glory of God in the face of Jesus Christ' (2 Corinthians 4:6 *ESV*). The unseen essence of God was displayed through Jesus the man[1].

John referred to Jesus as the 'One and Only' because never before or since has God been seen perfectly in one person. In Jesus, the 'outward and visible sign of an inward and invisible grace' – the grace and essence of God – was seen perfectly. There was and is nowhere else to look to find such completeness – only in Jesus.

When the Salvation Army's International Spiritual Life Commission produced its statement on Holy Communion[2], it included these words: 'Christ is the one true sacrament, and sacramental living – Christ living in us and through us – is at the heart of Christian holiness and discipleship.' Jesus is described as the one true sacrament because the divine and human natures are united fully in him – and fully only in him.

The unity of divine and human natures in Jesus is also described by Christians as the incarnation – God in man. When Christians speak of incarnational living they are often referring to people taking God's grace into a needy community – taking the light of God into dark places – living among those to whom they minister. The inner resources for such ventures

come from the presence of Christ in each life. This is God in man – not to the perfection of Christ – but with Christ supporting, guiding and sustaining. As Paul says, this is 'Christ in you, the *hope* of glory' (Colossians 1:27). Perfection not yet obtained (Philippians 3:12).

God in man – Christ in you – gives expression and substance to Christian living. It makes daily life sacramental. In God's hands, blessed and empowered by him, each life may become a sacrament – an outward and visible expression of an inward and invisible grace. No life will be the perfect example of sacramental living. Jesus alone is the one true sacrament, but the sincere offering of our lives to him in service is welcomed and sealed by his presence.

For some Salvationists the wearing of a uniform is an added visible witness to Christ's inner presence. It can be particularly meaningful. But the essence of Salvationism – of the Christian life – will always be found in the work of grace which the Lord does in each person.

The one true sacrament does not walk the earth as a man today. He asks us to make him visible by the way we live – in truth and grace.

SHARED REFLECTIONS

'In Jesus, the "outward and visible sign of an inward and invisible grace" – the grace and essence of God – was seen perfectly. There was and is no other place to look to find such completeness – only in Jesus.'

'God in man – Christ in you – gives expression and substance to Christian living. It makes daily life sacramental.'

'The one true sacrament does not walk the earth as a man today. He asks us to make him visible by the way we live – in truth and grace.'

PERSONAL RESPONSE
Consider how Christ asks us to help others see and find him today. In what ways can our lives give expression to Christ's presence in his world today?

20. ALL
Luke 16:13; John 12:32-33 and Colossians 3:11

From its earliest days, The Salvation Army has made wide use of the word
'all'. Its songs have spoken of wanting to give everything to God – 'All to
Jesus I surrender'[1], 'All my days and all my hours'[2], 'All there is of me, Lord'[3]
and, more recently, 'All that I am'[4]. Depth of personal relationship with Jesus
has been expressed with the words 'Christ is all, yes, all in all, my Christ
is all in all'[5]. Such words are in recognition of Jesus giving his 'all' for us –
confirmed in his death on the cross.

Since William Booth began his work among the poor of London's East End
in 1865, countries round the world have generally become more affluent.
Communities have grown in wealth and opportunity, though not in every case.
Challenges still remain. Often when people have become richer and more
self-sufficient, their love for God has waned. It becomes noticeable that the
most affluent countries usually show decline in commitment to a church or
belief in God. Paradoxically, it seems that the richer we get the less likely we
are to want to give our 'all' to God. Personal comfort takes precedence and
the sense of 'saved to serve' diminishes.

When this occurs, the emphasis in public worship often changes too. Songs
that speak of commitment are used less frequently, whereas those that thank
God for his goodness become more prominent. Naturally, there needs to be
a healthy balance of songs and readings in worship to keep our relationship
with God alive and interactive – but a move away from commitment also
takes Christians away from recognising that our true worship is found in the
way we live.

Although it enjoys its music, the Army was not born simply to enjoy public
worship in its citadels. The Army exists for those who don't yet know
Jesus and who need its ministry. Worship mustn't be divorced from reality.
When Jesus said that his being 'lifted up' would draw all people to him
(John 12:32), he was referring to his death on the Cross. He was not speaking
of being lifted up to Glory or by our thanksgiving and adulation. His focus was
on letting us know that he is with us in our suffering. He was lifted up on a
Cross – where he gave his all – so he could lift us up in our need. We must be
careful not to give an over-emphasis to our lifting Jesus up so that he seems
far away, beyond people's reach and everyday circumstances. Our worship
needs to be grounded in seeking his will for our daily living. God with us –
down to earth.

Yet his Lordship must not be minimised in our thinking – especially in an age of informality and individualism. To acknowledge Jesus as Lord is to accept our subjugation to him. This foundational approach must be at the heart of our relationship. The statement that 'Jesus is Lord of all or he is not Lord at all' says everything. A half-hearted response from us to Jesus' giving of his all – and therefore to his Lordship – is not only unworthy, but also futile. The benefit of what he offers – the joy of knowing we are fully his – will never be ours. It is all or nothing.

When Albert Orsborn wrote of placing our 'all' in the Master's hands, he concluded the verse with a prayer that spelt out what this meant – 'Resolved the whole of love's demands to give, for his dear sake'. We have returned to love being at the centre of everything – of our relationship with God and with everyone else. Love – standing supreme among the commandments – is both our gift and our calling.

To welcome Christ into our lives is to welcome the source of life, love and all goodness. To be truly in his hands is to be fully given over to him. It is to experience Paul's affirmation that 'Christ is all, and is in all' (Colossians 3:11). It is to be blessed beyond our deserving.

NOTES

IN HIS HANDS
CHAPTER 1
[1] The song 'My life must be Christ's broken bread' (*SASB* 610), shown at the beginning of the book, was written by Albert Orsborn, sixth General of The Salvation Army (1946-1954).

CHAPTER 3
[1] From Charles Wesley's hymn 'And can it be that I should gain…?' (*SASB* 241).

CHAPTER 4
[1] 'The blind man and Zacchaeus' chapter of *Jesus Through Middle Eastern Eyes*, Kenneth Bailey (SPCK Publishing), emphasises Jesus' readiness to become unpopular in order to help those who most needed him.

CHAPTER 5
[1] 'You can throw the whole weight of your anxieties upon him, for you are his personal concern' (1 Peter 5:7, *J.B. Phillips*).
[2] The concept of 'meetings' is further explained in the 'Call to Worship' chapter of *Called to be God's People*, by Robert Street, Salvation Books.

CHAPTER 6
[1] See the 'Serve Suffering Humanity' chapter of the 'In Purpose' booklet of the *One Army* series for a fuller consideration of the purpose behind Jesus' suffering.

CHAPTER 7
[1] See the 'Relationships' section of the 'In Christ' booklet of the *One Army* series which quotes St Augustine's prayer: 'You have created us for yourself, O Lord, and our hearts are restless until they find their rest in you.'

IN HIS NAME
CHAPTER 8
[1] The place of the mercy seat in Salvation Army life and worship is explained more fully in the 'Call to the Mercy Seat' chapter of *Called to be God's People*.

CHAPTER 11
[1] In his 'The Way and the Truth and the Life' chapter of *The Faith of a Christian*, Bishop John Austin Baker (Darton, Longman & Todd), former Chairman of the Church of England's Doctrine Commission, advocates the use of family meals to remember Christ's sacrifice.

[2] The International Spiritual Life Commission (ISLC) was set up by General Paul Rader to examine the heart of the Army's spiritual life. The book, *Called to be God's People*, presents its 12 calls to Salvationists.

[3] The ISLC provided 12 examples of ways in which fellowship meals can be used to enrich corporate spiritual life. They are listed on pages 65-66 of this book.

CHAPTER 12

[1] More detail can be found on this in Major John Read's Rationale on the Sacraments for the ISLC, printed in *Called to be God's People*. An extract from the rationale is on page 66.

[2] For fuller yet concise consideration of these issues, see the 'Second-century Sacraments' chapter of Ben Witherington's, *Making a Meal of It: Rethinking the Theology of The Lord's Supper* (Baylor University Press).

[3] The regularising of baptisms and 'love feasts' is seen in an instruction to the church at Smyrna from Ignatius of Antioch in about AD 110 – 'It is not permitted either to baptise or to hold a love feast without the bishop. But whatever he approves is acceptable to God, so that everything you do is secure and valid.'

[4] The word 'sacrament' was applied by Tertullian around AD 200.

[5] The earliest known references of the term 'transubstantiation' occurred in the 11th century – 1,000 years after the Lord's Supper – when it was used by a number of theologians, including Hildebert de Lavardin, Archbishop of Tours. It provoked fierce disagreement, especially from Berengar of Tours, Archdeacon of Angers, who challenged church leadership over its introduction.

CHAPTER 13

[1] Point 4 of the Army's Statement on Holy Communion, found in *Called to be God's People*, states: 'When Salvationists attend other Christian gatherings in which a form of Holy Communion is included, they may partake if they choose to do so and if the host church allows.' The full statement is on page 65.

[2] Writing to the chair of the ISLC, after enjoying his invitation to participate, Bishop John Austin Baker made a point of encouraging the Army to remember that it is 'free to express the faith and insight God has given you in any way that seems appropriate'. The 'Forward in Freedom!' introduction to the Commission's report, also found in *Called to be God's People*, gives similar encouragement to be creative in worship.

CHAPTER 14
[1] The booklet, *The Salvation Army in the Body of Christ*, is on pages 57-63, and gives clear, detailed information of the Army's understanding of its place within the Body of Christ.
[2] For further reading on the subject, see 'Notes on Baptism' by John Read, printed in *Called to be God's People*. The notes were part of the ISLC's deliberations.

IN HIS LIKENESS
CHAPTER 17
[1] See the song (*SASB* 610) in the front of this book.
[2] This definition of 'sacrament' was made by St Augustine in the fifth century. See also chapter 19.
[3] For further consideration of Jesus giving us authority to serve, see the 'Love and Discipleship' chapter of *Love – Right at the Heart*, and *Servant Leadership*, both published by The Salvation Army, International Headquarters, and written by Robert Street.

CHAPTER 18
[1] See chapter 12 and notes on chapter 12.
[2] See also the 'His presence in us' chapter of the 'In Holiness' *One Army* booklet.

CHAPTER 19
[1] *Holiness Unwrapped*, Robert Street, published by Australia Eastern Territory, gives emphasis to this, particularly in the 'To be like Jesus' section.
[2] See page 65.

CHAPTER 20
[1] 'All to Jesus I surrender' (*SASB* 636).
[2] 'All my days and all my hours' (*SASB* 566).
[3] 'All there is of me, Lord' (*SASB* 569).
[4] 'All that I am, all I can be' (*SASB* 568).
[5] 'I bring to thee my heart to fill' (*SASB* 588).

FURTHER READING

The Salvation Army in the Body of Christ
An Ecclesiological Statement

SUMMARY STATEMENT

1. The Body of Christ on earth (also referred to in this paper as the Church universal) comprises all believers in Jesus Christ as Saviour and Lord.
2. Believers stand in a spiritual relationship to one another, which is not dependent upon any particular church structure.
3. The Salvation Army, under the one Triune God, belongs to and is an expression of the Body of Christ on earth, the Church universal, and is a Christian denomination in permanent mission to the unconverted, called into and sustained in being by God.
4. Denominational diversity is not self-evidently contrary to God's will for his people.
5. Inter-denominational harmony and co-operation are to be actively pursued for they are valuable for the enriching of the life and witness of the Body of Christ in the world and therefore of each denomination.
6. The Salvation Army welcomes involvement with other Christians in the many lands where the Army is privileged to witness and serve.

AMPLIFIED STATEMENT

The Body of Christ on Earth

1. WE BELIEVE that the Church, the Body of Christ on earth, often referred to in the New Testament as 'the saints' (*hoi hagioi* – Ephesians 1:23), comprises all who are born not of natural descent, nor of human decision, or a husband's will, but born of God (John 1:13). The Church universal includes all who believe in the Lord Jesus Christ, confessing him as Saviour and Lord, and witnessing to that sacred commitment through loving mutual submission (Matthew 18:15-20; John 13:34-35; Ephesians 5:21) and sacrificial service (Mark 8:34; Matthew 20:25-28; John 13:1-17).

   WE DO NOT BELIEVE that the Church universal depends for its existence or validity upon any particular ecclesiastical structure, any particular form of worship, or any particular observance of ritual.

2. WE BELIEVE that the Church universal is the whole of the worshipping, witnessing Christian community throughout the centuries comprised of whatever groupings, large or small, accepted or persecuted, wealthy or poor, into which her members may have been gathered in the past or in the present.

WE DO NOT BELIEVE that an adequate definition of the Body of Christ on earth, the Church universal, can be confined in terms of ecclesiastical structure, but must rather be stated in terms of a spiritual relationship of grace that must find expression in all ecclesiastical structures. Members of the Body are those who are incorporate in Christ Jesus (Ephesians 1:1) and therefore reconciled to God through his Son. All such are in a spiritual relationship one with the other, which begins and continues regardless of externals, according to the prayer of Jesus that those who are his may be one (John 17:23). These words of Jesus ask for a oneness as is found in the oneness of Father, Son and Holy Spirit. This oneness is spiritual, not organizational.

3. WE BELIEVE that The Salvation Army belongs to, and is a particular communion of, the Church universal and a representative of the Body of Christ. Christ is the True Vine (John 15:1) and all believers are his living, fruit-bearing branches, exhorted by Scripture to live in Christlike unity (1 Corinthians 12:12).

WE DO NOT BELIEVE that any community made up of true followers of Christ can rightly be regarded as outside the Church universal, whatever their history, customs or practices when compared with those of other Christian communities. God alone knows those who are truly his (2 Timothy 2:19).

Denominational Variety

4. WE BELIEVE that God's dealings with his people are perfect according to his will, but that human responses are imperfect and prone to error. It may be God's dealings or fallible human responses to those dealings which have brought about the rich and varied denominational tapestry discernible today.

WE DO NOT BELIEVE that denominational or organizational variety can automatically and in every case be said to be contrary to God's will for his people.

5. WE BELIEVE that God raised up The Salvation Army according to his purposes for his glory and for the proclamation and demonstration of the gospel.

   WE DO NOT BELIEVE that The Salvation Army's existence as an independent and distinctive Christian church, having no formal, structural ties with other Christian churches, is an affront to the gospel of Jesus Christ or self-evidently contrary to God's will for the whole of his Body on earth.

6. WE BELIEVE that the practices of The Salvation Army have much in common with the practices of other churches, but that being raised up by God for a distinctive work, the Army has been led of God to adopt the following combination of characteristics:

   a. its emphasis upon personal religion and individual spiritual regeneration through faith in Christ leading in turn to a commitment in mission to seek to win others to Christ;
   b. its commitment to the unceasing proclamation of the gospel and its insistence that this gospel is for the whosoever;
   c. its teaching concerning sanctification and holy living;
   d. its teaching that the receiving of inward spiritual grace is not dependent upon any particular outward observance;
   e. its worldwide tradition of service (arising out of the compassionate love of Christ for all persons) without discrimination or preconditions, to the distressed, needy and marginalised, together with appropriate advocacy in the public domain on matters of social justice;
   f. its willingness to obey the 'great commission' of Jesus Christ, under the guidance of the Holy Spirit, by ongoing expansion of Salvationist witness and service into new countries, with a consequential celebration, with thanksgiving to God, of its internationalism;
   g. its preference for non-liturgical and flexible forms of worship, seeking to encourage spontaneity, for example in prayer and in spoken personal witness and testimony;
   h. its tradition of inviting public response to the presentation of the gospel message, and its use of the mercy seat for this and other spiritual purposes;
   i. its focus, in self-expression, on the biblical military metaphor of living in the world and of serving God as soldiers of Jesus Christ (2 Timothy 2:3; Ephesians 6:11-17);
   j. its requirement that adults and children wishing to become full members (soldiers and junior soldiers), and thereby wishing to make

a commitment to formal membership of the Body of Christ on earth, should publicly confess their faith in Jesus Christ as Saviour and Lord, the children making a simple statement of faith with promises as to lifestyle and the primary spiritual disciplines, and the adults entering into formal doctrinal and ethical commitments, the latter focusing on the sacredness of human relationships, but including also the personal disciplines of abstention from alcohol, tobacco, and non-medical use of addictive drugs;

k. its wearing of distinctive uniforms as a witness to belonging to Christ and as a signal of availability to others;

l. its encouragement into Salvation Army fellowship of those who do not wish to enter into the full commitment of soldiership (see j above), but are willing to become adherent members as a step in the journey of faith;

m. its recognition of the equal place within the Body of Christ of men and women in all aspects of Christian service, ministry and leadership including the holding of ecclesiological authority;

n. its readiness to use all forms of musical expression in worship and evangelism, and its encouragement in many cultures of the indigenisation of worship expressions and styles.

WE DO NOT BELIEVE it to be self-evidently God's will for his people in the Army that they cast aside in haste the leadings of God or the blessings of the years, but rather, in humility, to value them, learn from them, and harness and adapt them for ongoing relevance in future witness and service.

The Local Church

7. WE BELIEVE that just as the true Church universal comprises all who believe on the Lord Jesus Christ, so each denominational church comprises a community of believers who have in common the way the Lord, through the Holy Spirit, has dealt with them as a community. In turn, each denominational church comprises local congregations regularly meeting together for worship, fellowship and service in a relatively confined geographical location.

WE DO NOT BELIEVE that the validity of a denomination or its local congregations depends upon any particular ecclesiastical tradition, structure, hierarchy, form of worship, or ritual. Where even two or three gather in Christ's name there he is present (Matthew 18:20) with a presence no less real than that discerned in larger, more formal, ceremonial or liturgical settings.

The Army's Identity

8. WE BELIEVE that The Salvation Army is an international Christian church in permanent mission to the unconverted, and is an integral part of the Body of Christ like other Christian churches, and that the Army's local corps are local congregations like the local congregations of other Christian churches. The Army springs from the Methodist Revival and has remained unassimilated by any other denomination. Like other reformers before him, William Booth did not intentionally set out to found a new denomination. However, through the years Salvationism has moved on in its emerging self-perception, and in the perceptions of others, from being a para-church evangelistic revival movement (at first known as The Christian Mission) to being a Christian church with a permanent mission to the unsaved and the marginalised. Salvationists remain comfortable in being known simply as 'the Army', or a 'mission', or a 'movement', or for certain purposes as a 'charity'. All of these descriptors can be used alongside 'church'. With this multi-faceted identity the Army is welcomed to, and takes its place at, the ecumenical table at local, national and international levels.

WE DO NOT BELIEVE that The Salvation Army's history, structures, practices or beliefs permit it to be understood as anything other than a distinct Christian denomination with a purpose to fulfil and a calling to discharge under God. Similarly, its local corps cannot properly be understood unless seen primarily as local church congregations meeting regularly by grace and in Christ's name for worship, fellowship and service. Typically a local Army congregation will offer an integrated and holistic ministry, with both spiritual and social service dimensions, to the local population. Commissioned officers (both men and women) of The Salvation Army are duly ordained Christian leaders and ministers of the Christian gospel, called by God and empowered by the Holy Spirit to preach and teach biblical, apostolic truth (Acts 2:42), and to serve others in the name of Christ and for his sake.

The Army and Other Churches

9. WE BELIEVE that it is God's will that harmonious relations are built up and sustained, by divine grace, between Christians everywhere and between all Christian denominations including their local congregations. The Army's numerous and widespread contacts with other Christian communities around the world serve to enrich the Army and to enhance its understanding of the work of the Holy Spirit. For this reason the Army welcomes such contacts and seeks cordially to extend and deepen them.

WE DO NOT BELIEVE that narrowness or exclusiveness are consistent with God's will for his people, or that God has nothing to teach us by our sharing and co-operating with his people in other denominations. As in humility we learn from others, also we come to the ecumenical table ready to share whatever God in his wisdom has graciously bestowed upon the Army.

10. WE BELIEVE that every visible expression of the Church universal is endowed with its own blessings and strengths as gifts from God. We respect and admire those strengths, recognising too that because of human frailty every such expression, including The Salvation Army, has its imperfections.

WE DO NOT BELIEVE it is our task to comment negatively upon, or to undermine, the traditions of other denominations, and certainly not in relation to the sacraments (on which our distinctive, though not unique, position sees the whole of life as a sacrament with a calling from God to Salvationists to witness to a life of sanctity without formal sacraments). It is contrary to our practices to offer adverse comment upon the life of any denomination or local congregation. We seek to be careful not to belittle the doctrines or practices of any other Christian group. The Army places emphasis in its teaching not upon externals but upon the need for each believer personally to experience that inward spiritual grace to which an external observance testifies. We maintain that no external observance can rightly be said to be essential to salvation or to the receiving of divine grace and that the biblical truth is that we can meet with God and receive his grace anywhere at any time through faith. We recognise that external observances such as baptism and eucharist are used in many denominations as a means of grace. We believe that our calling into sanctity without sacraments is not a contradiction of the ways of other churches, but is something beautiful for Christ, to be held in creative tension with the equally beautiful, but very different, practices of other denominations. In the overall economy of God there are no inherent contradictions, but there are creative paradoxes.

11. WE BELIEVE that The Salvation Army was called into being by the will of God, is sustained in being by God's grace, and is empowered for obedience by the Holy Spirit. Its overriding purpose as encapsulated in the name God has given us – The Salvation Army – is therefore to strive to lead men and women and boys and girls into saving faith in Jesus Christ, working tirelessly and for Christ's sake, to develop them in holy living, that they might better serve suffering humanity while remaining unpolluted by the world (James 1:26-27).

WE DO NOT BELIEVE that we alone are called to these sacred and awesome tasks, and therefore we rejoice exceedingly because in other Christian churches we find co-workers for God.

Published by Salvation Books, 2008.

....

NOTE:

For Salvationist acceptance of the historic Christian creeds (The Apostles' Creed, The Nicene Creed, The Athanasian Creed) see *The Salvation Army Handbook of Doctrine* (Salvation Books, 2010).

**The International Spiritual Life Commission Statements
and other extracts from *Called to be God's People***

BAPTISM
A Statement on Baptism

AFTER full and careful consideration of The Salvation Army's understanding of, and approach to, the sacrament of water baptism, the International Spiritual Life Commission sets out the following points regarding the relationship between a soldier's swearing-in and water baptism.

1. Only those who confess Jesus Christ as Saviour and Lord may be considered for soldiership in The Salvation Army.
2. Such a confession is confirmed by the gracious presence of God the Holy Spirit in the life of the believer and includes the call to discipleship.
3. In accepting the call to discipleship Salvationists promise to continue to be responsive to the Holy Spirit and to seek to grow in grace.
4. They also express publicly their desire to fulfil membership of Christ's Church on earth as soldiers of The Salvation Army.
5. The Salvation Army rejoices in the truth that all who are in Christ are baptised into the one body by the Holy Spirit (1 Corinthians 12:13).
6. It believes, in accordance with Scripture, that 'there is one body and one Spirit … one Lord, one faith, one baptism; one God and Father of all, who is over all and through all and in all' (Ephesians 4:5-6).
7. The swearing-in of a soldier of The Salvation Army beneath the Trinitarian sign of the Army's flag acknowledges this truth.
8. It is a public response and witness to a life-changing encounter with Christ which has already taken place, as is the water baptism practised by some other Christians.
9. The Salvation Army acknowledges that there are many worthy ways of publicly witnessing to having been baptised into Christ's body by the Holy Spirit and expressing a desire to be his disciple.
10. The swearing-in of a soldier should be followed by a lifetime of continued obedient faith in Christ.

COMMUNION
A Statement on Holy Communion

AFTER full and careful consideration of The Salvation Army's understanding of, and approach to, the sacrament of Holy Communion*, the International Spiritual Life Commission sets out the following points:

1. God's grace is freely and readily accessible to all people at all times and in all places.
2. No particular outward observance is necessary to inward grace.
3. The Salvation Army believes that unity of the Spirit exists within diversity and rejoices in the freedom of the Spirit in expressions of worship.
4. When Salvationists attend other Christian gatherings in which a form of Holy Communion is included, they may partake if they choose to do so and if the host church allows.
5. Christ is the one true sacrament, and sacramental living – Christ living in us and through us – is at the heart of Christian holiness and discipleship.
6. Throughout its history The Salvation Army has kept Christ's atoning sacrifice at the centre of its corporate worship.
7. The Salvation Army rejoices in its freedom to celebrate Christ's real presence at all meals and in all meetings, and in its opportunity to explore in life together the significance of the simple meals shared by Jesus and his friends and by the first Christians.
8. Salvationists are encouraged to use the love feast and develop creative means of hallowing meals in home and corps with remembrance of the Lord's sacrificial love.
9. The Salvation Army encourages the development of resources for such events, which will vary according to culture, without ritualising particular words or actions.
10. In accordance with normal Salvation Army practice, such remembrances and celebrations, where observed, will not become established rituals, nor will frequency be prescribed.

* Terminology varies according to culture and denomination, and is not always interchangeable

FELLOWSHIP MEALS
A Statement on Fellowship Meals

RECOGNISING that every meal may be hallowed, whether in the home or with a congregation, there are strategic occasions when the planning

of a fellowship meal may especially enrich corporate spiritual life. Such occasions could include the following:
- In preparation for and during the Easter period.
- At the beginning of a mission or spiritual campaign.
- At a corps celebration such as an anniversary, a New Year's Eve watchnight service, or the opening of a new building.
- At a soldiers' meeting.
- For the pastoral care council (census board) or corps council, particularly when important decisions need to be made.
- For the launching of an annual appeal when the significance of work/ service being undertaken in Christ's name could be emphasised.
- Harvest thanksgiving.
- Between meetings when a meal is required and members of the congregation are unable to travel home to eat because of distance.
- When there has been a breakdown in relationships and healing is sought by reflecting on Christ's great act of reconciliation through the cross.
- Whenever it is thought that such a gathering would strengthen the spiritual life and wider fellowship of the corps or centre.
- Small group meetings, especially house groups, midweek meetings or (for example) at the conclusion of a recruits' preparation for soldiership course.
- Corps camps, fellowship weekends or retreats.

Two features of the common fellowship meal in the early New Testament Church were the scope for spontaneity and the element of charity, with the poor being included. These elements are also worth noting.

FROM 'RATIONALE ON THE SACRAMENTS'

The word 'sacrament' is not found in the Old or New Testaments, there is no evidence of a concept, such as the sacramental, which draws together baptism and the breaking of bread under one head. When further investigation is undertaken into the origin and derivation of the word 'sacrament' then the following emerges:
'Sacrament' derives from the Latin *sacramentum*. *Sacramentum* was the word used in the Vulgate to translate the Greek *mysterion*. *Mysterion* is never applied to baptism nor the breaking of bread. It is used definitively by Paul in Colossians. In Colossians 2:2 the *mysterion* of God, Paul says, 'is Christ'; in Colossians 1:27 Paul says the *mysterion* is 'Christ in you, the hope of glory'.

Paul used the word *mysterion* in order to contrast the secret rituals of the Hellenistic mystery religions, which created in the worshipper a sense of the transcendent and divine, with the mystery at the heart of the Christian faith which is 'Christ in you, the hope of glory'.

However, by the end of the second century, writers such as Tertullian were using the religious context of *mysterion* and *sacramentum* in order to compare the rituals of the Church – baptism and the breaking of bread – with the rituals of other religions, and to support the claim that the pagan mysteries were imitations or anticipations of the Christian mysteries. In this way *mysterion* and *sacramentum* came to lose their radical New Testament meaning and gained a meaning deriving from the mystery cults.

FROM 'CALL TO CELEBRATE CHRIST'S PRESENCE'

Perhaps we should give the Founder the last word:
'Let us do all that we do in remembrance of his dying love. Every act of our life ought to be religious. Every day ought to be a Sabbath in the sense of its being sacred and devoted to the glory of God, and every meal we take ought to be a sacrament. Look not only on the form and ceremonies; read your New Testament, not only with an eye on what I have told you, but settle it in your souls – that the Kingdom of God does not come by might nor by power; for the Kingdom of God is not meat and drink, it is not sacraments, nor ceremonials, not forms, not church attendance, not processions, not uniforms. The Kingdom of God is within you. It cometh not with observation. It is not what you can see or hear – the *essence* of it is not. Outside things may help you. They do help me very much. The countenances of my comrades help me, so do their songs, their faith, their devotion. The crash of a great big meeting, when hearts are yielded and souls are shouting the praises of God, helps me. But the power is not in these things. The Kingdom of God is righteousness, peace and joy in the Holy Ghost.'

one army

{ THE DVD }

one army

THE SALVATION ARMY

2A

{ THE DVD } IN CALLING
IN COVENANT
IN CHRIST
AN INTERNATIONAL TEACHING RESOURCE

WITH SUBTITLES:
ENGLISH, SPANISH, PORTUGUESE & FRENCH

Formatted for NTSC **DVD**

{ THE BOOK }

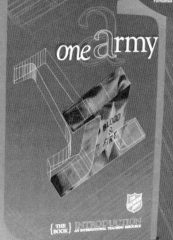

one army

{ THE BOOK } INTRODUCTION
AN INTERNATIONAL TEACHING RESOURCE

{ YOUTH BOOK }

{ LEADER'S MANUAL }

RESOURCES ALSO AVAILABLE ONLINE AT
www.salvationarmy.org/onearmy

one **army**

WRITTEN AND PRODUCED BY
ROBERT STREET, AUTHOR OF
IN THE MASTER'S HANDS

The youth script was written by
Nick Coke, who has also scripted
My Life in God's Hands,
a *One Army* youth production
to go alongside this book

One Army is an international teaching resource, written and translated for the more than 125 countries in which The Salvation Army is working. Its aim is to help the Army be what God calls it to be and to help its people become what God wants them to be.

Each of its 13 themed books includes materials for youth and young people, complemented by DVDs and additional suggestions in an accompanying leader's manual.

The series covers *One Army:*
INTRODUCTION
IN CALLING
IN COVENANT
IN CHRIST
IN TRUTH
IN PURPOSE
IN PRAYER
IN FELLOWSHIP
IN SERVICE
IN FAITH
IN HOLINESS
IN HOPE
IN LOVE

BOOKS AND FILMS are designed for personal use as well as for Sunday and weekday worship, house groups, café church, introducing newcomers to the fellowship and helping Salvationists worldwide enjoy and understand better their mission and unity of purpose in Christ.
The website facilitates live links at specific times for shared international study.

ABOUT THE AUTHOR

Robert Street was commissioned a Salvation Army officer with his wife, Janet, in 1969 and, in addition to corps leadership, served as Editor of *The War Cry* for 10 years and also as Editor-in-Chief, United Kingdom Territory. He was Principal, Booth College, London, UK, from 1997-2002 and served on the Army's International Doctrine Council from 2007, retiring as its chairman in 2014. Always keen to work alongside Christians from other denominations, he was chairman of both Norfolk and Suffolk Churches Together during the 1990s, when Divisional Commander, Anglia.

International experience came through service in Australia and appointments that involved oversight of work in the South Pacific and East Asia, as well as Europe, resulting in his seeing Salvation Army ministry in 50 countries. His chairmanship of the International Spiritual Life Commission prompted his writing a number of related books, including *Called to be God's People*, *Servant Leadership* and *Holiness Unwrapped*. He has devised, written and produced the international teaching resource *One Army* in retirement.

REFLECTIONS

REFLECTIONS